WORSHIP
WORD OF THE
DAY

A Devotional Journey through
the Language of Worship

Volume 1

ANTONIA PECOT

Worship Word of the Day

Published by Fresh Rain Music LLC, 5425 Peachtree Parkway
Peachtree Corners, GA 30092 (www.freshrainworship.com)

ISBN: 979-8-9997635-1-8 – (paperback)
ISBN: 979-8-9997635-0-1 – (ebook)
ISBN: 979-8-9997635-2-5 – (hardback)

Unless otherwise noted, Scripture quotations in this publication are taken from the New King James Version (NKJV)

Printed in the United States of America

TABLE OF CONTENTS

DEDICATION

To my Heavenly Father—
The One who chose me, carried me, and called me to worship.
From England to Jamaica, to Canada, to the United States, You have
written my story with the power of Your amazing grace.

From brokenness to confidence, from silence to song, You have
been my steady refuge and joy.
I feel Your pleasure when I worship, when I sing, and
when I have the privilege of leading others into Your presence
It is the highest honor of my life.

To my six amazing children and my grandchildren— The living proof of
God's goodness in my life. Love you always.

To my husband, R. Malachi—
Thank you for reflecting the love of 1 Corinthians 13.
You are inimitable.

To my friends, family, mentors, pastors and leaders I have had the Joy of
serving with—
Thank you for the steady light of your encouragement.

Your prayers and support along this journey,
your ministries and examples have helped me become the worshiper
and leader I am today.

And to you, dear reader—
May these words draw you closer to God who is worthy of every breath,
every song, every act of worship.

"Not to us, O Lord, not to us, but to your name be the glory,
because of your love and faithfulnes"
Psalms 115:1

FOREWORD

Words matter. They have depth of meaning. They shape our thoughts, stir our hearts, and frame how we see God and ourselves. In worship, words carry even greater weight, they become the vessels of our praise, the language of our prayers, the expression of our hearts, and the anchors of our faith.

In Worship Word of the Day, my friend Antonia Pecot has given the Body of Christ a beautiful gift: a devotional journey through twenty-six significant words that every believer should understand and embody.

Your worship is filled with words in your prayers and the lyrics you sing. You must know what the words mean if you want to not simply sing-along. With a gentle, guiding voice, Antonia invites you to pause and consider the depth of these words and how they can shape your relationship with the Lord.

Each day's reflection is more than a definition; it is an invitation. An invitation to draw close to Christ, to bless the Lord with genuine gratitude, to live in joyful obedience to His commandments, and to dwell in His presence as your home and refuge.

The Scriptures, prayers, and personal applications she provides will help you learn the meaning of these words and experience their power in your daily worship and walk with God. Speak and sing them with the richness of their meaning.

I believe this devotional will strengthen your worship, deepen your love for God, and awaken a richer vocabulary of praise in your heart. I pray that as you read, you will not just know these words, you will live them.

Thank you, Antonia, for this tool, which gives us vocabulary for our love for Jesus and deepens our worship.

—LaMar Boschman, author, mentor, and worship pioneer.

LaMarBoschman.com

From the Author

I Love Words! Words are powerful. They inspire, create, build, and transform. In fact, the very foundation of our existence began with words. "In the beginning was the Word, and the Word was with God, and the Word was God." (John 1:1) God used words to create the heavens and the earth, to bring life into being. As a singer and songwriter, I know the weight of every single word. Every lyric matters because words carry weight and meaning. They can encourage someone's heart and even change a life. Words don't just create—they can destroy too. The Word of God tells us, " Death and life are in the power of the tongue..." (Proverbs 18:21)

Words do more than communicate ideas—they carry the very heart and spirit of the one who speaks. When that person is filled with the Holy Spirit, every word becomes infused with life and power. The spirit behind the words reveals the source within. Jesus said, "Out of the abundance of the heart the mouth speaks" (Matthew 12:34). Harsh or critical words release fear, anger, or judgment, but words spoken in love transform the atmosphere—they bring peace, healing and connection.

If a person speaks with love, then they will experience the spirit of love behind the words. What we say has the power to either build up or tear down. A careless word can wound deeply, but a kind one can heal a broken soul. So, choose your words wisely. Speak life, speak love, and speak truth, speak God's word because it contains it all, and it truly makes a difference. Whether in conversation, through a song, or even on social media, your words matter more than you realize. Above all, desire that every word we speak be filled and guided by the Holy Spirit.

Study the words of life to show yourself approved by God, and you will be a blessing to others. Because words are not just sounds—they are life-giving! Your words are activators, they are seeds you plant. What kind of seeds are you planting today?

Speak Life always,

Antonia

My Mission:

" To cultivate the heart of true worship, in every believer."

WELCOME TO
WORSHIP WORD OF THE DAY!
BY ANTONIA PECOT

This daily devotional is about diving into single common words that we, as believers, often use in our faith journey. We frequently hear these words in our vocabulary and songs, but do we stop to think about their meaning and how they apply to our lives personally?

Each devotional Word starts with a letter of the alphabet; it serves as a moment to pause, reflect, and think about each Word as it relates to our personal relationship and daily connection with God. These moments are called **Selah Moments**. In those beautiful moments, my prayer is that God will powerfully reveal Himself and give us that personal revelation for our lives. Because the Psalms are a book of poetry and music, "Selah" is a term thought to be a musical pause or a musical interlude. David was a powerful example of a worshipper. He is described in the Word as "a man after God's own heart," a musician and a poet. In the Psalms, the word **"Selah"** is used 71 times.

As believers, we are all a part of God's beautiful design and His heavenly orchestra. We all have a specific part to play; we each have different instruments, gifts, talents, and a vital role in the kingdom of God and the musical masterpiece He has created. We all must pay attention to our Heavenly Father, the Divine Conductor. He will direct us and keep us together in unity as it relates to timing, our rhythm, unique expression and detail of our lives. He will guide us into those moments when the spot light shines on us together, when we solo; when we pause, let the music breathe and we "rest" in Him. You are an instrument in His hand. The "Selah" moment in the music of life is just as important as the rhythm.

In this fast-paced life, it is so important for us to stop, focus and meditate on God's presence and allow His word to reverberate and echo loudly in our hearts. To stop and listen intently to His music. Silence allows us to hear His whisper. Sometimes we rush through our prayers, reading, or worship, but Selah invites us to pause, reflect and linger a little longer, and receive the rain of His presence and let it soak in. It's an invitation "Be still, and know that I am God; " (Psalm 46:10)

Each day, we will explore one Word commonly found in our spiritual vernacular and worship songs. We will dive into the meaning, biblical context, a Selah Moment, a Declaration, prayer and song. My prayer is that each Word will deepen our daily walk with God.

Feel free to share your own thoughts or reflections on each Word and how it impacts you. Build a space where these powerful words come alive in our everyday faith!

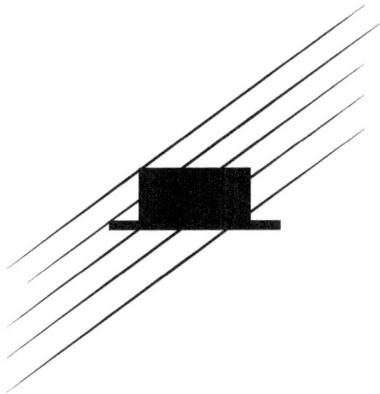

GOD IS LOOKING FOR THOSE WHO WILL WORSHIP HIM IN SPIRIT AND TRUTH.

FOR OUR WORSHIP TO BE "TRUE," IT MUST BE POWERED BY THE HOLY SPIRIT AND BASED ON THE TRUTH OF GOD'S WORD.

TRUE WORSHIP MUST BE CHRIST-CENTERED NOT SELF-CENTERED.

ABIDE

A

"Abide in Me, and I in you. As the branch cannot bear fruit by itself unless it abides in the vine, neither can you, unless you abide in Me."

John 15:4 NKJV

Understanding the Word

To abide means to remain, dwell, or stay connected. It is living in continual awareness, communication and communion with God, relying on His presence and His Word for guidance, strength, and sustenance.

Selah Moment

Abiding in Christ is the foundation of a fruitful and victorious life in Christ. John 15:5 says, "I am the vine, you are the branches. He who abides in Me, and I in him, bears much fruit; for without Me you can do nothing. The Vine represents Christ, and just as a branch is connected to the vine, and receives life, nourishment and strength, we receive the same from our relationship and our connection to the Lord. To abide means to dwell consistently in His love, allow His Word to saturate our hearts, and remain steadfast in faith even through life's challenges. When we abide, we rest in His presence and allow His Spirit to transform us. This abiding relationship enables us to bear the fruit of the Spirit. Not just a little bit, but much fruit! The fruit of love, joy, peace, patience, kindness, goodness, faithfulness, gentleness, and self-control. This is the really good fruit that we can share and be a blessing to others; it equips us to reflect His character in the world. It is a daily commitment and a lifelong journey of walking in close communion with the Father.

Declaration

I choose to abide in Christ today and every day, drawing strength, peace, and purpose from His presence. His Word is my lamp and the light that guides me; He restores my soul, as I remain steadfast in His love. I am totally and completely dependent on the Lord.

Prayer

Father, thank You for Your invitation to abide in You. Teach me always to be aware of your presence in my life and to stay connected to You through every season of life. Let Your Word dwell richly in my heart and let Your Holy Spirit guide my steps. I am totally dependent on You, Lord. Help me walk in the power of Your amazing love and bear the abundant fruit You desire. The kind of fruit that feeds your people and glorifies Your name. In Your Powerful name I pray, Amen.

Listen to this:
"Abide" by Aaron Williams

"Pause and Ponder"

Today is the day to focus on abiding in Christ, enjoying His presence, reflecting on His Word, and drawing strength by staying connected to Him. The awareness of His presence is what makes the difference in our lives. Write down how you have noticed the Lord in your day.

BLESS

B

"Bless the Lord, O my soul, and all that is within me, bless His holy name!"

Psalm 103:1 NKJV

Understanding the Word

The word "bless" is a powerful word that we use often as believers. But what does it mean? To bless God means to honor Him with our hearts full of reverence, gratitude, and adoration. It's our way of acknowledging who He is and His greatness. We bless Him through our praise, our worship, our thanksgiving, and by choosing to live in a way that brings Him glory. To bless others is to show favor and kindness in a way that reflects the heart of God.

Selah Moment

True blessings flow from a connection to a real relationship with Christ. When we seek Him first, when we choose His ways over our own, that's when we begin to walk in the fullness of what it means to be blessed by God. It is more than just a good feeling or a word we just throw around when things go our way. Being blessed means we are walking in the favor of God and in awareness of His presence in our lives. Being aligned with His purpose and fully embracing His plan. When we are blessed, it shows up in many ways: peace in the middle of chaos, joy that doesn't make sense, a quiet contentment that fills our soul, and the kind of well-being that goes deeper than material things.

It is not about stuff, it is about significance. A truly blessed life is rooted in obedience to God, fueled by prayer, shaped by worship, and poured out in service. We are blessed to be a blessing! God has empowered us to bless others and give the priestly blessing in Numbers 6:24-26 "The Lord bless you and keep you; the Lord make His face shine upon you and be gracious to you; the Lord lift His countenance upon you and give you peace." To bless someone is to speak life over them, to call forth God's goodness. We bless people with our words, our love, our time, our prayers. When we bless others, we are reflecting God's character by speaking life, extending grace, and desiring their good. Being a blessing to others is living a lifestyle of generosity, encouragement, and love. When we say "I am blessed," or we call others a "blessing," it all points back to the One who blesses us beyond measure, not just so we can have, but so we can give.

Declaration

I praise my God from whom all blessings flow! I will bless the Lord at all times; His praise will continually be in my mouth. I will speak life and not death; hope and encouragement to all those around me. I am blessed to be a blessing.

Prayer

Heavenly Father, I bless Your holy name for Your goodness, faithfulness, and love. Thank You for blessing me with Your peace, provision, protection and most of all Your presence. Teach me to live as a blessing to others, reflecting Your kindness and grace in all I do. May my words and actions glorify You and bring hope to those around me. In Jesus name, Amen.

Listen to this:
"Blessed" by Fred Hammond

"Pause and Ponder"

Take a moment today to find songs that speak about blessing the Lord. Let it lead you into heartfelt worship as you pour out your praise. Then, look for a chance to bless someone else through a kind word, a prayer, or a simple act of love that reflects the heart of God.

_____

_____

_____

_____

_____

_____

_____

_____

_____

_____

COMMANDMENTS

C

"If you love Me, keep My commandments."

John 14:15 NKJV

Understanding the Word

Commandments are divine instructions given by God as guidelines that lead us into a life of righteousness, love, worship, and holy living. The Ten Commandments were delivered to Moses as the core principles for every believer to live by. It reveals God's magnificent nature and His desire for how we are to relate to Him and to others. The first four commandments teach us how to honor and worship God, always putting Him first. The remaining six guide us in how to treat others with respect, dignity, integrity, and love. Together, they form the foundation of a life that pleases God and blesses those around us.

Selah Moment

The first commandment sets the foundation for the other nine: "You shall have **no** other gods before Me" (Exodus 20:3). This command is the heartbeat of true worship. When we put God first above all else, everything else falls into place. Obedience, love, priorities, and relationships fall into divine alignment when He is in His rightful place. God's commandments bring freedom, clarity, peace, and purpose. In the New Testament, Jesus affirmed and fulfilled those commandments. He spoke of the greatest commandment. When we obey this one, we obey them all: "Love the Lord your God with all your heart, soul, and mind, and love your neighbor as yourself."(Matthew 22:37-40) Let this be the focus of our lives as believers–when we obey this commandment, we walk in power, victory, love and favor with God and man.

Declaration

I love the Lord with all my heart, soul, mind, and strength. I choose to love others as I love myself. I express that love by walking in His ways. His commandments are not a burden to me; they are a blessing. They lead me into truth, anchor me in peace, and draw me into a deeper, more intimate relationship with Him.

Prayer

Father God, thank You for Your commandments, which lead me in the way of life. I choose today to put You first, to worship You with my whole heart, and to walk in obedience as an act of love. Help me to see Your commands not as restrictions, but as invitations to live in harmony with Your perfect will. Teach me to delight in Your Word and follow it faithfully. In Jesus name, Amen.

Listen to this:
"Yes (Obedience)" by David & Nicole Binion

"Pause and Ponder"

Today, take time to read and write out the Ten Commandments. Meditate and memorize them. Pay close attention to the first four commandments, and how we are to demonstrate honor to the Most High God. Let His commandments be the foundational guide for your everyday life.

_____

_____

_____

_____

_____

_____

_____

_____

_____

BE MORE AWARE OF THE
PRESENCE OF GOD
MORE THAN THE ABSENCE
OF ANYTHING!

DWELL

D

"He who dwells in the secret place of the Most High shall abide under the shadow of the Almighty."

Psalm 91:1 NKJV

Understanding the Word

Dwell means to live in, remain, or stay somewhere continuously; to take up residence. To dwell in the secret place means to make the presence of God our home, a place we never leave; it's about resting in His love, relying on His strength, and remaining rooted in His truth. It's a daily decision to stay connected, to listen, to worship, and to walk closely with Him.

Selah Moment

God's presence is definitely the place to be! In His presence is fullness of joy. He desires a relationship with us and that we make His presence our constant place of refuge. When we dwell in Him, we choose to let our hearts rest in Him, no matter what is happening around us. David said, "One thing I have desired of the LORD, that will I seek after; that I may dwell in the house of the LORD all the days of my life, to behold the beauty of the LORD, and to inquire in His temple" Psalm 27:4. NKJV

To dwell in God's presence is to live with a deep awareness of His nearness. It is not an occasional visit; it is about making Him your permanent home. It is a place where we experience the power of His presence; where our soul finds peace, rest, safety, and a sense of belonging.

Dwelling in God's presence involves staying connected to Him through prayer, worship, and meditation on His Word. When we choose to sin, we have chosen to disconnect and not listen to His voice. When we stay connected, His peace becomes our peace, and His strength becomes our strength. He gives us a daily invitation to be fully present with Him, to let Him fill our hearts and minds and be embraced by His love. Psalms 84:1 says "How lovely is your dwelling place, LORD Almighty!"

Declaration

This is my ONE desire. I choose to dwell in the presence of the Most High. His nearness is my refuge, His shadow is my shelter, and His presence is my peace. No matter where I go or what I face, I remain rooted in Him. I am never alone. My heart has found its home in the presence of God.

Prayer

Father God, thank You for Your invitation to dwell in the secret place of Your presence. In a world that pulls me in every direction, You remain constant, the same yesterday, today and forever. Your name is a strong tower. You are my shelter, my safe place, my fortress, my anchor of peace and protection. Teach me to hide in You always, not just in moments of worship, but in the everyday rhythms of life. Let Your presence be the air I breathe and the song that I sing. May I live each day fully aware of who You are in my life. In Jesus name, Amen.

Listen to this:
"Psalm 42" by Tori Kelly

"Pause and Ponder"

Practice mindfulness today, take time to "pay attention" to the presence of the Lord. Stay connected and tuned in to His voice because He is always there. Let Him be your ONE desire— dwell in Him and let His presence be your Hiding Place. What does it mean to you to make the Lord your Hiding Place?

_____

_____

_____

_____

_____

_____

_____

_____

_____

EXCELLENT

E

"O Lord, our Lord, how excellent is Your name in all the earth, Who have set Your glory above the heavens!"

Psalm 8:1 NKJV

Understanding the Word

Excellent refers to something outstanding in nature; it is superior and of the highest quality. When we speak of God's excellence, we are acknowledging that He is infinitely perfect, awesome in power, wisdom, love, and majesty.

Selah Moment

Everything God does is excellent! This is seen all throughout creation–from the vastness of the universe to the smallest details of creation and the complexity of our bodies and our lives. His works are magnificent and unparalleled. His flawless character and mighty works reflect a power that is brilliant and unmatched. Everything He does is marked by His signature of greatness, beauty, and purpose. Truly, there is no one like our God. When we declare that God is excellent, we are praising His superior nature, there is no one and nothing that compares to Him.

Worshipping God is a call to honor Him with excellence in our lives, whether in our words, our work, or our acts of love and service. Philippians 4:8 "Finally, brothers and sisters, whatever is true, whatever is noble, whatever is right, whatever is pure, whatever is lovely, whatever is admirable if anything is excellent or praiseworthy—think about such things.

Excellence should always be our goal. The Father wants us to be excellent in our thoughts as well as our deeds. Romans 16:19 declares, "Be excellent in what is good. Be innocent of evil". Actively pursue and practice things that are righteous, noble, and life-giving, with purity of heart.

Declaration

I am created in the image of an excellent God. Today, I will strive for excellence in all I do, offering my very best as a reflection of His glory. I walk in the excellence of His wisdom, power, strength, and love, knowing that His Spirit empowers me to honor Him with my life.

Prayer

Oh Lord my God, You are excellent in all Your ways. Your name is majestic, and your works are beyond comparison. From the splendor of the heavens to the wonders of Your grace, You reveal a glory that surpasses understanding. Help me to live in awe of who You are every day and to reflect Your excellence in every area of my life. Let my worship be pure, my words be full of truth, and my actions be guided by love. Father, I desire to give You my best not out of duty, but out of deep devotion. May Your excellence shine through me today and always. In Jesus name, Amen.

Listen to this:
"Oh Lord How Excellent"
by New Jersey Mass Choir

Praise His excellent name and let His greatness inspire your worship. Focus on the beauty of nature, the good and the perfect gifts and all the blessings in your life. As you meditate on God's excellence today, write what you are thankful for that shows His greatness in your life; how has God been excellent in your life this week? Don't forget to encourage someone today with words of excellence (text, email, or speak a kind truth).

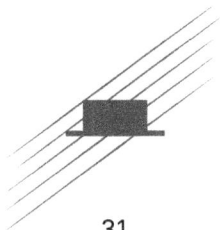

_____

_____

_____

_____

_____

_____

_____

_____

FAITHFULNESS

F

"Through the Lord's mercies we are not consumed, because His compassions fail not. They are new every morning; Great is Your faithfulness."

Lamentations 3:22-23 NKJV

Understanding the Word

Faithfulness is a deep, unwavering loyalty, a steadfast commitment that doesn't shift with circumstances or emotions. God's faithfulness is perfect and unchanging. He is completely reliable, always true to His Word, and never fails to keep His promises. No matter what we face, He remains present, constant, and trustworthy, a faithful Father who will never abandon His own.

Selah Moment

My favorite attribute and what I love the most about God is His faithfulness. He has proven Himself trustworthy, over and over again in my life. His faithfulness is a cornerstone of our hope. From generation to generation, He is the same yesterday, today and forever. He has never failed to fulfill His Word. Especially in those moments, when we face trials or feel uncertain, we can hold onto the truth that God is always faithful. He continues to demonstrate that His love is steadfast, His promises are sure, and His care for us is constant.

Remembering God's faithfulness gives us confidence to face the future and the strength to stand firm in our faith. Just as God is faithful, we are called to live with faithfulness in our relationship with Him and others.

This means being committed, loyal, and dependable, reflecting His character in our actions. By trusting in God's faithfulness, and being faithful to Him, we are empowered to remain steady, no matter what life may bring.

Declaration

Great is the faithfulness of God, and His promises are yes and amen! I trust in His unwavering love and believe that He is working all things together for my good. Today, I rest in the assurance of His faithfulness and choose to reflect His steadfast love in all I do. By His Spirit, I will consistently walk with a heart that is steady, loyal, and full of purpose.

Prayer

Faithful Father, I thank You for Your steadfast love that never fails and Your mercies that are new every morning. You are constant when everything around me changes. You are true when all else feels uncertain. Teach me to rest in the security of Your promises and to walk daily in the confidence of Your Word. Let Your faithfulness be the foundation of my trust, the strength of my worship, and the anchor of my soul. Help me reflect Your loyalty and love in how I live, love, and lead.

In Jesus name, Amen.

Listen to this:
"Great Is Thy Faithfulness"
by Carrie Underwood & Cece Winans

"Pause and Ponder"

Write out your testimony. How have you seen God's faithfulness in your life, and how have you been faithful in return? Share it with someone today.

THE KING ON THE THRONE
SHOULD ALWAYS BE
IN THE MIDDLE OF OUR
WORSHIP AND THE CENTRAL
FOCUS OF OUR ADORATION

IT IS CRITICAL THAT THE
GREAT SOVEREIGN ONE
IS AT THE CENTER OF OUR
LYRICS, OUR PRAYERS,
AND OUR SERMONS.

GOD IS THE FOCAL POINT
OF EVERYTHING.

WONDER
Exploring the Mysteries of God
LaMar Boschman

GLADNESS

G

*"Serve the Lord with gladness;
Come before His presence
with singing"*

Psalm 100:2 NKJV

Understanding the Word

Gladness is a feeling of deep joy and delight; a sense of happiness and gratitude that comes from the inside out. In the context of worship, gladness is the joy that comes from being in God's presence and recognizing His goodness in our lives.

Selah Moment

David declared, "I was glad when they said to me, 'Let us go to the house of the Lord.'" Can you imagine what David was feeling when he said that? He spoke from his personal experience of the goodness of God. He had so many testimonies of what God had done for him. This wasn't just casual excitement; it was gladness that overflowed from deep within. The kind of gladness you cannot fake; the kind that lights up your face, a smile that lifts the atmosphere around you. Gladness is contagious!

God calls us to worship and to serve Him with this kind of gladness. But where does that gladness come from? It flows from an intimate relationship, personal testimonies, the awareness of His presence, His faithfulness, and His unfailing love. This kind of joy doesn't waver with our circumstances. It is anchored in His truth, His goodness, and faith in a Holy God who never ever changes.

To worship with gladness is to celebrate who God is, even in the midst of trials. It is choosing joy when the conditions don't make sense. It is responding to His presence with heartfelt praise, because we know His boundless mercy, His amazing grace, and that He is a God who never breaks His promises. When we choose to focus on God's blessings and His presence, this is a powerful expression of faith as we respond to Him with joyful praise.

Declaration

I will serve the Lord with gladness, my heart overflows with joy today. I choose to celebrate God's goodness and embrace the joy that comes from knowing Him. I am so grateful for His blessings, and His gladness fills my soul and inspires my worship. My life is a song of praise, and I walk in the joy of His presence.

Prayer

Heavenly Father, thank You for the gift of gladness that springs from Your presence. You are my joy, my song, and the reason I celebrate. Even when life brings challenges, I choose to serve You with a heart full of joy, knowing that Your goodness never fails. Let my worship be filled with gladness that reflects the wonder of who You are. Fill my spirit with joy today, and let it overflow into everything I do. May my life be a light that points others to Your love and the joy of walking with You. In Jesus name, Amen.

Listen to this:
"This is the Day" by Lakewood

Rejoice in the Lord today and let His gladness be your strength and delight. Start your day with a worship song that makes your heart smile. Carry the song in your heart throughout the day— hum it, sing it, or whisper the lyrics when you're tempted to complain.

HALLELUJAH

H

After these things, I heard a loud voice of
a great multitude in heaven saying
'Allelujah! Salvation and glory
and honor belong to the Lord our God."

Revelation 19:1 NKJV

Understanding the Word

Hallelujah is a Hebrew word composed of two parts:
- "Hallel"- a command meaning "praise!"
- "Yah" is a shortened form of Yahweh, the sacred name of God in Hebrew.

Together, Hallelujah means: "Praise Yahweh" or "Praise the Lord." What is so amazing is that the word "Hallelujah" is the same in every language. This is not just a coincidence, but it was divinely orchestrated by God.

Selah Moment

Hallelujah is more than just a word; it's a powerful declaration of God's worthiness and a call to worship Him with our whole hearts. It is expressing the highest form of adoration and praise to God for who He is! When we say "Hallelujah," we are lifting the name of the Lord and acknowledging His power, glory, faithfulness, and unfailing love for what He has done and for who He is.

This Word is often sung and used in moments of deep gratitude, celebration, and reverence for God's greatness. Praising God with a heartfelt Hallelujah shifts our focus from our struggles to His power and love. It reminds us of His sovereignty and fills us with hope and joy, knowing that He reigns overall.

No matter what we are going through, there is always a reason to say Hallelujah because God is good, He is worthy of our praise, and His power and love are undeniable.

Declaration

I praise the Lord with my whole heart, for He is good, and His love endures forever. He is worthy of my highest praise, and I celebrate His greatness and faithfulness in my life. I choose to lift His name, rejoicing in the hope and joy He brings. My heart is full of praise and joyful Hallelujahs as I declare His goodness today and always! HalleluYAH!

Prayer

Lord, my Hallelujah belongs to you alone! I give You the highest praise for Your love, power, and faithfulness. Thank You for being my Creator, my Savior, and my constant source of strength. I am in awe of Your majesty and grateful for Your presence in my life. Fill my heart with a spirit of praise, no matter my circumstances, and help me to always remember Your goodness. May my life be a song of "Hallelujah" that brings glory and honor to Your name always.

In Jesus name, Amen.

Listen to this:
"You Deserve It" by JJ Hairston

Lift a heartfelt, loud "Hallelujah" over and over again today. He is worthy of the highest praise! Let your praise be a joyful offering to the Lord. Sing with all your heart the one-word hymn "Hallelujah" by Andrae Crouch and sing the song "My Hallelujah Belongs to You." Let it be a Hallelujah Day!

IDOLATRY

I

"You shall have NO other gods before me.
"You shall not make for yourself an image
in the form of anything in heaven
above or on the earth. You shall not
bow down to them or worship them;
for I, the Lord your God,
am a jealous God.

Exodus 20:3-4 NKJV

Understanding the Word

Idolatry is worshipping or giving ultimate value to something or someone other than the one true God. It is loving anything or anyone in place of God. When we worship, it means to hold in high regard and esteem, to show reverence, adoration, honor, and to bow down before. It is placing something else above God in our hearts, affections, or priorities. We were created for one purpose: to love the Lord our God with our ALL.

Selah Moment

Back in the Old Testament, idols were obvious, visible statues and images like the golden calf in Exodus 32. But in our modern world, idolatry often looks different. Today's "idols" might be money, success, fame, relationships, status, or even ourselves. Our culture constantly pushes us to worship celebrities, achievements, and platforms. Just think of shows like American Idol, The Voice, or even award shows like the Grammys, where the world celebrates people as if they were gods.

But our Heavenly Father is clear: "You shall have no other gods before Me" (Exodus 20:3). We were created to worship Him and Him alone, to give Him all glory, honor, and devotion. Idolatry isn't just bowing to a statue.

It happens anytime we give something, or someone, more of our trust, focus, or affection than we give to God. What makes it so deceptive is how quietly it can take root in our lives. Sometimes, it's the endless scroll on social media that eats away at our time with Him. Sometimes, it is ambition that drives us harder than our desire for His presence. Sometimes, it is craving the approval of people more than the approval of God. Idolatry is subtle, but it is very real.

That's why we need to constantly pause and check our hearts and ask ourselves; what do I treasure the most? What consumes my thoughts, my time, my energy? Like David prayed in Psalm 139:23-24, let us pray, "Search me, O God, and know my heart, see if there is any wicked way in me, and lead me in the way everlasting." God doesn't call us to give Him first place because He needs our worship. He calls us because we need Him. He designed us to be fully connected to Him. The moment we try to do life in our own strength, we will always fall short. Jesus said it plainly: "Apart from Me, you can do nothing" John 15:5.

But when we tear down the idols, when we surrender the things that compete for His place in our hearts, and put Him first, this is when we experience true peace, real provision, His protection, His power, and we walk in our God-given purpose.

Declaration

I worship the one true and living God; there is no one and nothing above Him in my life. I will not bow to the idols of this world, nor will I place anything before Him. My heart is fully devoted to the Lord, who is holy, faithful, and jealous for me. I choose to honor Him alone with my worship, my loyalty, and my life. He alone is worthy.

Prayer

Lord, search my heart and reveal anything that I've placed above You. Forgive me for the times I have allowed idols to take Your rightful place. I surrender every false god, whether it's fear, approval, possessions, or pride, and I choose to worship You alone. Be the center of my life, and lead me in Your truth always. In Jesus name, Amen.

Listen to this:
"No One"
by Chandler Moore & Elevation Worship

"Pause and Ponder"

Think about it, what are some of the idols in our world today? Take a moment to meditate and answer this question: How do I keep the idols out of my life and demonstrate that God IS my first and highest priority?

_____

_____

_____

_____

_____

_____

_____

_____

_____

A TRUE WORSHIPER
REFLECTS AND DEFLECTS
ALL GLORY, HONOR,
GRATITUDE AND WORSHIP
BACK TO GOD.

WE ARE NOT MEANT TO
RETAIN GOD'S GLORY,
AS IT TURNS INTO PRIDE
AND CORRUPTS OUR
CHARACTER AND LIFE.

JOY

J

" The joy of the Lord is your strength."

Nehemiah 8:10 NKJV

Understanding the Word

Joy is a deep, abiding sense of gratitude that comes from knowing God and being in His presence. Joy is not just being happy, but it is a spiritual position centered and rooted in God's love, promises, and faithfulness. Unlike fleeting emotions, joy is steady and enduring, even in difficult times, because it is based on our relationship with God.

Selah Moment

Joy is a gift from God. Jesus set the example for us. Hebrews 12:2 says, "Looking unto Jesus, the author and finisher of our faith, who for the joy that was set before Him endured the cross, despising the shame, and has sat down at the right hand of the throne of God." While life can bring both blessings and challenges, joy helps us to look beyond and see hope, to see what God wants us to see. Joy remains because it comes from trusting in God's goodness and His plans. Joy fuels our faith, gives us strength, and helps us persevere through life's circumstances. It is a reminder that God is with us, and His presence is the source of our true contentment.

As we walk in the energy of joy, we become a reflection of God's light to others. Joy is contagious; it draws people closer to the love of God in us and offers hope in a world that often lacks lasting peace. When we choose joy, we choose to focus on God's promises rather than on our problems, and we experience His peace and strength in return.

Declaration

The joy of the Lord is my strength. I rejoice in His love, His promises, and His presence in my life. I don't find joy in what's happening around me, but in who God is and the unchanging connection I have with Him. I choose joy daily, trusting in God's goodness and letting His light shine through me.

Prayer

Lord, thank You for the gift of joy that comes from knowing You. Help me to be rooted in this joy, no matter what I face, knowing that Your presence is with me. Let Your joy be my strength and my anchor, guiding me through both joyful and challenging times. May my life be a testament to the joy and peace that only comes when we abide in You. Help me to share this joy with others, drawing them closer to You.
In Jesus name, Amen.

Listen to this:
"Joy" by Vashawn Mitchell

"Pause and Ponder"

Let the joy of the Lord fill your heart today, and allow it to energize you and lift your spirit, bringing peace and joy to those around you. What are your thoughts about this "joy" God has given you, and how do you stay filled?

_____

_____

_____

_____

_____

_____

_____

_____

_____

KING

K

"For the Lord Most High is awesome;
He is King over all the earth...
Sing praises to our King,
sing praises! For God is King
of all the earth"

Psalm 47:2-6 NKJV

Understanding the Word

A king is the male head of a royal family and the chief ruler of a kingdom or nation. Kings typically rule for life and often inherit their position. Psalms 47:1 is clear: "For God is the King of all the earth."

His title is also "King of kings", which proclaims that He is the source of all power and has ultimate authority. He is the supreme ruler reigning over all creation; over all earthly kings and rulers, He possesses ultimate power and wisdom. God is sovereign, and His kingship is eternal and perfect. Unlike earthly kings, He reigns with justice, mercy, and unending love. He deserves our complete devotion and reverence.

Selah Moment

God is King! When we come to the realization of who He is, His nature, His goodness, His power and love, we cannot help but bow our hearts before Him. We can come boldly before Him, knowing that He is not only our King but also our loving Father. He is not a tyrant, but an amazing God who loves us with an everlasting love. As our King, He is our protector and provider, ruling with justice and compassion. His authority is not slavery, but liberating, bringing order, purpose, and peace into our lives. Psalms 95:3 "For the Lord is the great God, the great King above all gods."

When we submit to God as our King, we are acknowledging His wisdom over our own. We can trust that His plans for us are good, even when we don't fully understand them. God's kingship calls us to live as His royal and loyal followers, honoring His Word, seeking His will, and reflecting His character in our daily lives. The beauty of God as King is that, even though He holds all power, He invites us into a personal relationship with Him. Our King knows us intimately and cares about every aspect of our lives.

Declaration

God is MY King. He reigns over my life with wisdom, justice, and love. I submit to His authority, and I trust in His plans for me. I honor Him with my heart, my actions, and I worship Him, knowing that He is good, and He is perfect in all of His ways.

Prayer

You are the King of Kings! I bow before You with reverence and gratitude. Thank You for ruling with justice, mercy, and love. Help me to honor You as my King, submitting to Your will and trusting in Your perfect plan for my life. Teach me to live in a way that reflects who You are and Your kingdom values. Let my life bring You honor and glory always. Thank You for being both my King and my Father. Let Your kingdom come, and Your will be done in my life, on the earth and in me, as it is in heaven. In Jesus name, Amen.

Listen to this:
"That's My King" by Cece Winans

"Pause and Ponder"

Answer these questions. Does my life bring honor to my King?

Am I making decisions that reflect His justice, mercy, and love?

Am I living as a citizen of His Kingdom or a captive to my own ambitions?

_____

_____

_____

_____

_____

_____

_____

_____

_____

LOVE

L

And we have known and believed
the love that God has for us.
God is love, and he who abides
in love abides in God,
and God in him.

1 John 4:16 NKJV

Understanding the Word

The Bible is so clear about the definition of love. 1 John 4:8 "Whoever does not love does not know God, because God is love." God **is** love, and real love comes from Him. Love is the essence of who He is. He expresses pure and undefiled love that is selfless, sacrificial, and eternal. His love is not just an emotion but a covenant in action. He demonstrated His love when He gave His Son as a ransom for us. Through His generosity, He set an example for us to follow and a call for us to love one another.

1 Corinthians 13 shows us what true love really looks like and how we are to identify and express it to one another: "Love is patient, love is kind. It does not envy, it does not boast, it is not proud. It always protects, always trusts, always hopes, always perseveres. Love never fails."(vs. 4–8)

Selah Moment

Love is the heartbeat of our faith and the very foundation of true worship. It is not a feeling; it is trusting the character of God Himself. His love is pure, unwavering, and unconditional. His love never fails. John 3:16 says "For God so loved the world that He gave His only Son…" God desired a relationship with humanity, and the greatest expression of that love was revealed through Jesus Christ, who laid down His life for us on the cross.

As believers, we are known by our love; who we love, what we love and how we display love. He commands us to love the Lord with all our heart, soul, mind and strength and love our neighbors as we love ourselves.

This divine love is not something we earn or deserve; it is freely given, a reflection of God's very nature. When we experience God's love, it transforms us and compels us to respond by loving others. This love is active, forgiving, enduring and without fear. It reaches beyond our emotions and into every part of our being, in our thought life, our words and our deeds.

Declaration

I am deeply loved by God, and His love has transformed my heart. I will love Him with all that I am; with all my heart, soul, mind and strength and I will reflect His love to others and myself. His perfect love casts out all my fears and fills me with peace, joy, and purpose.

Prayer

Lord, thank You for Your unfailing love. Help me to receive it fully and to trust in You and your power to transform my life. Teach me to love You with my all and to love others as You have loved me. Let my life be a daily reflection of that love, bringing hope and light to those around me because Your love never fails.

In Jesus name, Amen.

Listen to this:
"One Thing Remains" by Israel Houghton

"Pause and Ponder"

Be intentional as you share God's love today. Ask Him to show you someone who needs to experience His love through you, a person who may need an encouraging word, a listening ear, forgiveness, or just a simple act of kindness. God's love is expressed when you also pray for others...who are you praying for today?

_____

_____

_____

_____

_____

_____

_____

_____

OUR HIGHEST CALLING IS
TO KNOW GOD,
TO LOVE HIM, AND
TO SERVE HIM

NOT MERELY WITH SONGS
OR OUTWARD EXPRESSIONS
BUT WITH OUR ENTIRE BEING

WORSHIP IS THE NATURAL
RESPONSE OF A HEART
CAPTIVATED BY
GOD'S LOVE

MAGNIFY

M

"Oh, magnify the Lord with me, and let us exalt His name together!"

Psalm 34:3 NKJV

Understanding the Word

Magnify means to make something appear larger or more prominent. When you look through a magnifying glass, you see the details you could not see before. In worship, when we magnify the Lord, it is about elevating His greatness, focusing on His power, and giving Him the glory He deserves. It is not making God greater (He is already great), but it is shifting our perspective, focusing on the details of His nature and who He is, so we can proclaim His glory and majesty with greater clarity.

Selah Moment

To magnify God is to make Him the center of our lives and to give our full attention to His presence, majesty, goodness, and sovereignty, making Him preeminent in everything we do. In a world full of distractions and challenges, magnifying God reminds us of His all-encompassing power and love. There is a song that says, "Turn your eyes upon Jesus, look full in His wonderful face and the things of earth will go strangely dim, in the light of His glory and grace." Turning our eyes to Him allows everything else in life to be less important. When we make God bigger in our perspective, we allow His truth to overshadow our fears, doubts, and worries. King David encouraged the people of God to magnify the Lord.

We magnify Him by lifting our voices. David initiated collective worship, he said, "Oh magnify the Lord and let us exalt His name together." This is how we fight our battles as believers; we magnify and praise the name of the Lord; we focus on His power, we declare that He is the Most High, and we will see the victory because of our faith in Him. Worshiping God in this way aligns our hearts with His and shifts our perspective from our problems, from self-centeredness, to Christ-centeredness. It is an intentional act of exalting God in our thoughts, words, and actions, declaring that He is greater than anything we could ever face. 1 John 4:4 says "...greater is He that is in you, than he that is in the world."

Declaration

I choose to magnify the Lord in all I do. I will focus on His character, not on the problem, but on Him as the Solution! He is a BIG God. He is great and greatly to be praised. My heart and mind are focused on His greatness, and I will proclaim His power, love, and faithfulness above all else in my life.

Prayer

Lord, I magnify Your name today. You are greater than anything I face, and Your power and love are beyond measure. Teach me to see You clearly and to elevate Your name in every area of my life. Help me to live in a way that draws others to join in magnifying Your goodness and glory. In Jesus' name, Amen.

Listen to this:
"Oh Magnify the Lord" by Jonathan Butler

"Pause and Ponder"

Today is the day to reflect on God's greatness. Magnify the Lord with your words, thoughts, actions, and focus. Focus on His greatness more than your circumstances. The more you make room in your heart and mind, the larger He appears in your life and to those around you. Declare His goodness out loud and magnify His name.

NAME

N

"The name of the Lord is a strong tower;
the righteous run to it and are safe."

Proverbs 18:10 NKJV

Understanding the Word

A name is a word or set of words by which a person is known, addressed, or referred to. A "name" often connects to your reputation, character, and what you are good at. It reflects the nature, integrity, and authority of a person. When we call on the Name of the Lord, we're not just saying a word, we are calling on His nature, His power, His faithfulness, His strength, His reputation, and His character.

Selah Moment

The nature and the goodness of our Heavenly Father is so vast, so limitless, that no single name could ever capture the fullness of who He is. That's why, throughout Scripture, He reveals Himself through more than 650 names and titles that describe who He is, each one unveiling a different facet of His character, His power, and His heart toward us. His name, "Great I AM," covers everything. When Moses asked God, Who shall I say sent me, God said to Moses, tell them... "I AM has sent me to you.." When Mary gave birth, Isaiah 9:6 says, "For unto us a child is born, to us a Son is given...and His name will be called Wonderful Counselor, Mighty God, Everlasting Father, Prince of Peace." God's Name isn't just a label; it is a revelation of who He is. He is Jehovah Jireh (Provider), Jehovah Shalom (Peace), El Shaddai (All-Sufficient One), and so much more. His Name carries weight, His presence carries His power and promise.

When we are born, we are given a name, and we are known by that name for the rest of our lives. The Bible speaks about the value of a good name, Proverbs 22:1 states, "A good name is more desirable than great riches; to be esteemed is better than silver or gold," according to Proverbs 22:1. Through the power of a good name, you can make a difference, a powerful impact on the world and a lasting legacy that extends beyond our own lifetime. Proverbs 18:10 says, "The name of the LORD is a strong tower; the righteous run to it and are safe." It is in His name we find safety, healing, deliverance, and purpose through the power of His Name. His name is above all names, and at the sound of that name, every knee will bow and every tongue will confess that He is Lord.

Declaration

The Name of the Lord is my strong tower, my place of safety and provision. I will run under that name when I am afraid. I will put my trust in Him. The power of His name gives me authority, peace, and all the promises of God. His Name is my strength, my peace, my joy, my healing, my deliverance, my abundant life and in Him I am always secure.

Prayer

Father, thank You for revealing Yourself through Your Name. Your Name is holy, powerful, and personal. I run to it and find peace. Teach me to honor Your Name in all I say and do. Let the Name of Jesus be ever on my lips and alive in my heart. In His mighty Name I pray, Amen.

Listen to this:
"Speak the Name" by Charity Gayle

Speak His Name intentionally today. When you pray, declare His Name based on what you need: My Provider, Healer, Peace, Shepherd, Savior... Say it with faith. Speak the Name over your body and soul, your family and friends. There's protection, power, and peace in His Name. List all the names of God and what they mean to you.

Also, think about this: what does your name mean? If you don't know the meaning, look it up and write it down.

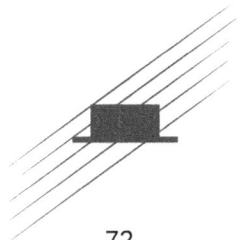

_____

_____

_____

_____

_____

_____

_____

_____

OBEDIENCE

O

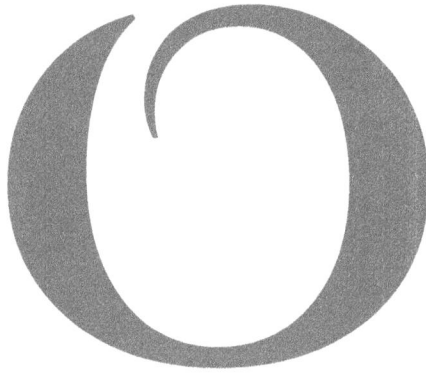

"...if you diligently obey the voice of the Lord your God, to observe carefully all His commandments which I command you today, that the Lord your God will set you high above all nations of the earth."

Deuteronomy 28:1 NKJV

Understanding the Word

Obedience is the act of submitting to authority or following instructions willingly and faithfully. Obedience to God isn't just following rules; it is the posture of the heart, a humble, trusting attitude of surrender to God's will, His Word, and His ways. It is about responding to God's voice out of love, trust, and reverence. In both the Old and New Testaments, obedience is directly connected to covenant, blessing, faith, and love. It's a response born out of a relationship, not legalism.

Selah Moment

Obedience to God's word is the highest form of worship. Obedience says: "I firmly believe in Your word and I choose to say, Yes Lord." It turns belief into action and faith into works. It is an act of full surrender and dependence, which is at the heart of true worship. It declares, "God, I trust You more than my feelings and my fears." In 1 Samuel 15:22, we see that God honors obedience even more than sacrifice. "To obey is better than sacrifice," means that God prioritizes obedience from a humble heart over perfect worship services, religious rituals or offerings. Jesus modeled perfect obedience, even to the point of death on a cross. As we walk in obedience, even in small things, we are aligning ourselves with heaven's purpose and creating space for God's blessing and presence to move freely in our lives.

Declaration

I choose to walk in obedience today, not out of obligation, but out of love for my Savior. His ways are perfect, and I trust His direction for my life. Obedience is my offering. I delight to do Your will, O God. I trust that every step of faith leads me closer to Your heart and deeper into my purpose.

Prayer

Lord, help me to obey You with a willing and joyful heart. Teach me to trust Your Word more than my own understanding. Give me the courage to follow You fully, even when it's hard or inconvenient. I want my life to be a living expression of worship through obedience.
In Jesus name, Amen.

Listen to this:
"Trust and Obey" by Dan Lopez

"Pause and Ponder"

Obedience always leads to peace, clarity, and fruitfulness.

How can I reflect my love for the Lord more deeply through practical obedience today and everyday?

_____

_____

_____

_____

_____

_____

_____

_____

_____

_____

GOD IS LOOKING FOR THOSE
WHO WILL
WORSHIP HIM
IN SPIRIT AND TRUTH.

FOR OUR WORSHIP TO BE
"TRUE," IT MUST BE POWERED
BY THE HOLY SPIRIT
AND BASED ON THE
TRUTH OF GOD'S WORD.

TRUE WORSHIP IS
CHRIST-CENTERED
NOT SELF-CENTERED.

PRAISE

P

"Let everything that has breath praise the Lord. Praise the Lord!"

Psalm 150:6 NKJV

Understanding the Word

Praise means to express admiration, honor, and gratitude for someone's character and actions. When we praise people, it is a way to recognize the good and encourage others. Praising God is an active declaration and appreciation of His goodness, greatness, His attributes and His holiness. It is our response to who He is and what He has done.

Selah Moment

Praise is a powerful expression of admiration that brings us closer to God as we recognize who He is and what He has done. Praise allows us to focus on His goodness; to draw us into a deeper understanding of His nature, reminding us that He is worthy of our gratitude and our full attention. Through the power of praise, we take our eyes off our challenges, and we recognize God's power, love, mercy and goodness.

Praise is our weapon, because when we praise, Psalms 22:3 says, "He inhabits the praises of His people," and when His presence comes, the enemy scatters. Prison doors are open, blinded eyes see; as we lift up His name through our praise, miracles happen. Praise is about who God is, His majesty, wisdom, and sovereignty. It is an act of gratitude and humility, acknowledging that He alone deserves glory and honor.

In Scripture, we see many forms of praise: singing, shouting, dancing, lifting hands, and even silently meditating on His goodness. Praise is not just a Sunday morning activity; it's a daily practice that renews our faith and shifts our hearts toward God. Whether we're in joy or struggle, praise reminds us that God is worthy of our worship and that He is ever-present, guiding and sustaining us through it all.

Declaration

I will praise the Lord at all times! His praise will continually be in my mouth. He alone is worthy of all honor, and I choose to lift His name above all else in my life. I celebrate His goodness, His faithfulness, and His unconditional love.

Prayer

Lord, I come before You with a heart full of praise. Thank You for Your goodness, Your power, and Your endless love. Help me to live a lifestyle of praise, focusing on Your perfection and Your power, and not my circumstances. May my words, thoughts, and actions honor You, be pleasing in Your sight and may my heart overflow with gratitude always. Lord, I lift Your name on high, for You alone are worthy of all praise, honor and glory. In Jesus name, Amen.

Listen to this:
"Praise" by Elevation Worship
(feat. Brandon Lake, Chris Brown & Chandler Moore)

"Pause and Ponder"

Take a moment for a "praise break" today. Thank God for His goodness in your life, whether through a song, a dance, a prayer, or quiet reflection on His greatness.
Even in tough times, finding reasons to show gratitude and praise invites God's presence and joy into our lives.

Take time to share with someone what you are praising God for. Write down everything you are praising God for and what you are grateful for.

_____

_____

_____

_____

_____

_____

_____

_____

QUIETNESS

Q

"In returning and rest you shall be saved;
in quietness and confidence shall
be your strength."

Isaiah 30:15 NKJV

Understanding the Word

Quietness is more than the absence of noise; it is a sacred stillness. It is a rare and sacred gift. In Psalms 23, David said, " He leads me beside the still waters." Just picture yourself beside a tranquil lake, its surface perfectly still, like glass reflecting the morning light. The air is hushed. No ripples, no rush, just peace. In that moment, you become more aware of something much deeper: God is near. This kind of quietness is not empty, it is full of beauty and clarity, and the weight of God's presence.

Selah Moment

In this noisy world we live in, silence often feels uncomfortable. We often rush to fill it with words, music, busyness, demands, or inner chatter. God treasures the quiet. It is in the stillness that He moves most powerfully. It is in the calm that we hear His unmistakable whispers, free from fear, distraction or the need to strive. It is not just the absence of sound, but the presence of peace. Psalms 46:10 says "Be still, and know that I am God." Quietness is the surrender of the soul that builds a holy confidence. It often refers to a posture of the heart that is at rest, fully dependent on God's undeniable nearness. It is the quietness that comes when we lay down our need to control and rest in God's sovereignty.

Isaiah 32:17 declares "The work of righteousness will be peace, and the effect of righteousness, quietness and assurance forever." When we cultivate quietness in our hearts, we create space to hear from God, to be refreshed in His presence, and to regain spiritual strength. Enjoy a moment with the Lord. Slow down, silence the distractions, turn off your notifications and simply be with Him. His voice is not heard in loud fanfare but in the stillness of our souls.

Declaration

I am so glad that the LORD is my Shepherd; I have everything I need. He makes me lie down in green pastures, He leads me beside still waters, and He restores my soul. I choose quietness over the chaos. In the stillness is where I find my strength, and in God's presence, I find peace and contentment. My soul rests in Him, and I am renewed every day.

Prayer

Father, thank You for the gift of quietness and the strength that You give. Teach me to "be still" so I can know that I know, You alone are God. In the stillness, help me to rest and trust You in the silence. Quiet my anxious thoughts and calm my heart in the green pastures of Your presence. Help me to learn to embrace the peace that is only found in Your presence alone. In Jesus name, Amen.

Listen to this:
"Quiet Time with God"
1 Hour Instrumental Worship / Prayer Music

"Pause and Ponder"

Quiet yourself today. Find a peaceful place, maybe in your car, your closet…close your eyes, even if just for a few moments, invite God to meet you there. Focus on His presence. Let His peace fill your heart. "Be still" and you will know that He is God. Reverence His presence today and everyday. How does your heart feel?

_____

_____

_____

_____

_____

_____

_____

_____

REJOICE

R

"Rejoice in the Lord always.
Again I will say,
Rejoice!"

Philippians 4:4 NKJV

Understanding the Word

When we add the prefix "RE" to a root word, it gives the meaning of returning to a previous state, starting over, or doing something again with renewed strength or focus. Even though the root word comes from the word "joy", it shares the same root of gladness, delight, or joy. Rejoice means to experience or express joy again or to return to a state of joy. In the context of worship and faith, to rejoice in the Lord is to find deep and abiding joy in God's presence, His promises, and His faithfulness, regardless of our circumstances, over and over again.

Selah Moment

When Paul says "Rejoice," he is literally saying, "Keep returning to the joy of the Lord and do it again and again!" It is not based on circumstances; it's a decision to come back to the joy found in God's presence and promises; and in who God is and what He has done for us. Rejoicing is not just an emotional feeling; it is a choice to celebrate His goodness and faithfulness, even when life is hard. Paul gives us a command from the Lord to rejoice in the Lord, not just sometimes but always. This is a reminder to us that our joy is not dependent on what is going on in our lives or how we feel, but on our relationship with a loving, unchanging God who loves us and wants the best for us.

When we rejoice, we shift our focus from our problems to God's power. We are reminded that He is in control and that His plans are always good for us. When we rejoice, it brings hope, strength, and peace, filling our hearts with God's light. It's an act of faith and worship that acknowledges the greatness of our God.

Declaration

My joy is not rooted in my circumstances but in God's faithfulness and unchanging love. He has made me glad, so I choose to rejoice in the Lord today. No matter what comes my way, I will celebrate His goodness and trust in His perfect plan. He has filled my heart with His joy. As the Magnificat, the song of Mary proclaims, "My soul magnifies the Lord, and my spirit rejoices in God my Savior." His joy overflows from my heart, bringing hope and light to those around me.

Prayer

Heavenly Father, thank You for being my source of joy and strength, and for giving me a reason to rejoice every day. Help me to always keep my eyes on You, even in challenging times. Thank You for Your faithfulness and love. Help me to rejoice always, as Your Word says, and to pray without ceasing. In everything I will give thanks to You; for this is Your will for my life in Christ Jesus. Let my life be a reflection of the fullness of joy in Your presence. Use me, Lord, to spread this light of joy to others. In Jesus name, Amen.

Listen to this:
"Again I Say Rejoice" by Israel Houghton

"Pause and Ponder"

No matter what you're facing today, take a moment to REjoice— not because everything is perfect, but because God is still good. Has God done or is He still doing a lot of "RE's" in your life?

Take time to write them down. (Example—REnew, REfresh, REvitalize, REstore...etc) Celebrate His goodness!

_____

_____

_____

_____

_____

_____

_____

_____

PRAISE IS GRATITUDE IN
MOTION—
LOVE THAT REFUSES TO
REMAIN SILENT.

IT IS THE SACRED VEHICLE
THAT CARRIES US BEYOND
THE OUTER COURTS,

INTO THE HOLY PLACE
OF INTIMACY WITH
OUR CREATOR.

SELAH

S

"But You, Oh Lord, are a shield for me, My glory and the One who lifts up my head. I cried to the Lord with my voice and He heard me from His holy hill." Selah

Psalm 3:3-4 NIV

Understanding the Word

Selah is a Hebrew word found frequently in the Psalms, appearing over 70 times. Most scholars believe Selah indicates a rest, a moment of silence, an invitation to reflect, or an intentional pause to contemplate what has just been said.

It is a pause that creates tension or anticipation, allowing the listener to process what has been said. It could also be described as a "pregnant pause" designed to intentionally create and carry a significant meaning that often suggests something is about to happen or has just happened. It is also used to emphasize a deeper time of reflection, worship and reverence.

Selah Moment

Selah is one of those fascinating mysteries in the Word. In the Psalms, David, the worship leader, song writer and poet, used this word "Selah" to:

1. Create Space for Reflection
"Selah" invites the reader or worshipper to pause and meditate on what God is saying.

2. Emphasize a Profound Truth
"Selah" often follows a powerful declaration about God's character, mercy, or justice. David used it to draw attention to His divine nature or a promise worth meditating on.

3. As a Worship Cue

Since David was a worship leader and musician, "Selah" was likely a musical cue signaling an instrumental break or for the people to lift their voices.

4. Invite Stillness and Reverence

God often speaks in stillness. To "Be Still" and experience His presence and hear His voice. David knew this and used "Selah" as a sacred moment, making room for God to speak, for the heart to listen, for faith to rise and His Spirit to move.

In this fast-paced world, "Selah" invites us to slow down and pay attention to God's presence, His promises, and His goodness; not rush past His profound truths, but to marinate on His word and let it resonate within us. It's saying, "Don't rush past this moment, think about it." David said, "My soul, wait silently for God alone, For my expectation is from Him" Psalms 62:5.

Declaration

Today, I choose to patiently pause and reflect on God's faithfulness and love. In the silence, the sacred becomes clearer and my heart is more in tuned. Stillness sharpens my spiritual eyes and ears and softens my heart to receive. I am renewed and have become stronger. I take time every day to meditate on His word and allow His truth to fill my heart and mind. I rest in His powerful presence, knowing He is faithful, full of wonder and majesty, and He is worthy of my worship.

Prayer

Father, how awesome it is to stop everything and focus on You. To sense the power of your presence; to wait on You with joyful anticipation. Help me to pause and to slow down to feel Your peace and reflect on who You are. Help me to always remember Your consistent love and faithfulness. Teach me to worship You deeply and intentionally, letting Your truth fill my heart and shape my life. May each Selah moment draw me closer to You, strengthening my faith and filling me with Your passion and purpose. In Jesus name, Amen.

Listen to this:
"Quiet in His Presence"
Soaking Worship Instrumental
Prayer, Devotional, Meditation and Relaxation

"Pause and Ponder"

Turn off the TV, radio, all the noise of life and embrace the beauty in silence. "Selah," meditate on His word, in the stillness of the moment and soak in His presence. Worship your God with intention and respond thoughtfully to His Word. Be still and know who He is... What is He saying to you today?

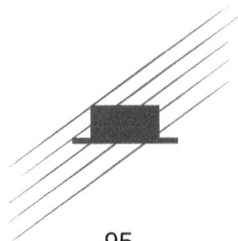

TRUST

T

"Trust in the Lord with all your heart and lean not to your own understanding; in all your ways acknowledge Him, and He will direct your paths."

Proverbs 3:5-6 NKJV

Understanding the Word

Trust means to rely on, to place total confidence, faith, and dependence in someone or something. When we trust a person, we trust their character, their ability, and we believe that what they say or do will be consistent with who they are.

We feel a sense of safety. There is only one who can be completely trusted. When we put our trust in God, we also surrender our fears, doubts, and uncertainties to Him, believing that He is faithful, loving, and in control of our lives.

Selah Moment

Trust flows from the heart. When trust is partnered with love, there is no fear or doubt. 1 John 4:8 says "There is no fear in love. But perfect love drives out fear." Trusting God is foundational to a life of faith. To trust Him is to let go of the need to control and understand every detail, and to rely on God's wisdom and unfailing love. Often, life leads us into situations that we don't understand, and we don't know what to do. It is in these moments that the power of God shines bright. We can always trust God when we remember that His ways are higher than ours, and His plans are always for our ultimate good, even if we can't see the outcome.

Trusting God means believing in Who He IS. He will always guide, protect, and provide in His perfect timing.

It means believing His promises, even through the struggle and the pain of life. It's not a one-time decision but a daily choice to stand on His promises, lean into His presence, and believe that He is always with you. Trust is an act of worship because it declares our confidence in who He is and His unchanging character.

Declaration

I trust in the Lord with ALL my heart. He knows my path, He guides my steps, and He holds my future in His hands. I release all my worries and fears and choose to rely on His perfect character that never changes. He is faithful even when I am faithless. He is in control, and I am safe.

Prayer

Lord, thank You for being trustworthy. Help me to release my fears and lean fully into Your promises. When I face uncertainties, I pray that I will always remember Your faithfulness and trust wholeheartedly in You. Teach me to rest in Your presence and your promises, knowing that You hold my life in Your hands. May my trust in You continue to grow stronger each day, and may my life be a testimony to Your amazing love. In Jesus name, Amen.

Listen to this:
"Trust In God" by Elevation Worship
(feat. Chris Brown)

"Pause and Ponder"

Today, take a moment to identify and write down any fears, regrets, worries and doubts you are carrying and release them to the Father.

Declare your trust in the Lord with all your heart, and sing to Him "I trust in YOU Lord."

_____

_____

_____

_____

_____

_____

_____

_____

_____

UNDERSTANDING

U

"For God is the King of all the earth;
Sing praises with understanding.
God reigns over the nations;
God sits on His holy throne."

Psalm 47:7-8 NKJV

Understanding the Word

Understanding means the ability to perceive, discern, and comprehend truth. Context is absolutely essential in gaining a true understanding. Words, actions, and events can have drastically different meanings depending on the surrounding information. Context leads to truth and clarifies meaning, and knowing the big picture helps you apply knowledge accurately. It is not just intellectual knowledge, but understanding comes through personal experience and insight given by God.

Selah Moment:

There is a big difference between knowing God and knowing about God; between relationship and personal experience versus mere information. The Apostle Paul in Philippians 3:10 said, "...that I may know Him and the power of His resurrection and the fellowship of His sufferings, being conformed to His death." Paul expressed a deep desire for an intimate, experiential knowledge of Christ. We must dedicate our intellect to learning about God. As we pursue knowledge of God, we will grow in the understanding of His nature and who He is. It is a powerful way to demonstrate our love. We cannot lean on our own understanding because our understanding is flawed and tainted with sin. His wisdom is infinite, so He wants us to seek His understanding over our own.

When we ask God for understanding, it is a demonstration of our faith, our dependence on Him and our desire to see life through His eyes. It is a posture of humility that leads to wisdom, clarity, and peace. True understanding comes from the Holy Spirit, who teaches us and guides us into all truth and deepens our relationship with the Lord. God has a plan for us, and understanding, drastically improves when we see the big picture and the context. In Ephesians 1:17-19 Paul prays, "…that God would grant believers the spirit of wisdom and revelation, so we may know Him and to more fully understand the hope of our calling."

The more we seek the Lord and rely on Him who is all-knowing, the more confidently we can live out our calling. God is looking for those who will worship Him in Spirit and truth. The Holy Spirit helps us to understand truth— and it is that truth that empowers us to authentically live a lifestyle of worship that pleases our Heavenly Father. God wants us to praise and to worship Him with the understanding that He is sovereign and supreme. He rules the whole earth with wisdom and justice and is worthy of our worship.

Declaration

I will diligently seek the Lord for understanding above my own. I love His wisdom because it is perfect, and I trust Him to guide my steps. I am not limited by what I know, because the Spirit of God gives me clarity and insight. I walk in His truth and He makes my path clear. My heart is open, and my mind is renewed by His Word.

Prayer

Heavenly Father, give me Your knowledge, wisdom and understanding that I may worship your Name with fresh revelation. I thank You that Your ways are higher than mine. As Ephesians 1:18 says, I am praying that the eyes of my heart may be enlightened in order that I may know the hope to which He has called me, and the riches of His glorious inheritance in His holy people. Help me to see with spiritual eyes and to discern Your will in every situation. Where I am uncertain, give me clarity. Where I am confused, speak Your truth to my heart oh God. I desire to love you with **all** my mind. In Jesus Name – Amen

Listen to this:
"Get Understanding"
Written by Antonia Pecot / Suno

What does it mean to trust Him completely and to totally lean on His wisdom and not on your own strength? Let your life reflect His insight, and may you walk in the peace that comes from knowing He holds all power in His hands. In Jesus name, Amen.

REAL WORSHIP IS NOT ABOUT
PERFECT WORDS, POLISHED
PERFORMANCES, AND RELIGIOUS
HABITS.

IT IS A SINCERE HEART
THAT SEEKS AFTER GOD,
EVEN IN BROKENNESS
AND WEAKNESS.

GOD IS NOT LOOKING FOR
THOSE WHO GO THROUGH
THE MOTIONS,
BUT FOR THOSE WHO
WORSHIP FROM A GENUINE
RELATIONSHIP, NOT A
REHEARSED ROUTINE

VICTORY

V

*"But thanks be to God, who gives us
the victory through our Lord Jesus Christ."*

1 Corinthians 15:57 NKJV

Understanding the Word

The dictionary defines victory as an act of defeating an enemy or opponent in a battle, game, or competition. Victory signifies a state of triumph and superiority; an achievement of success in a struggle or conflict, gaining a higher, more advantageous position.

In the spiritual sense, it means triumph through God over sin, fear, trials, and the enemy of our souls. It is not just a moment of success, but a life marked by overcoming. It is through faith in Christ that we have true victory!

Selah Moment

True victory is found in the finished work of Christ on the cross and His resurrection, which has secured eternal life and freedom for all who believe. As believers, we are not fighting for victory; we are fighting from a position of victory. Jesus has already won the ultimate battle for us. This truth empowers us to face every challenge, trial, and spiritual opposition with confidence, knowing the outcome has already been settled in Christ. Victory doesn't always look like immediate success. Sometimes it looks like peace in the middle of a storm, strength when we're weak, or hope when things look hopeless. But no matter the season, God promises that we are "more than conquerors" through Him.

Walking in victory means living in alignment with God's truth, standing firm on His promises, and trusting Him completely—even when circumstances are hard. Our victory brings glory to God and points others to the power of His name.

Declaration

I am more than a conqueror through Christ. The battle is not mine; I have victory because He fights my battles. No matter what I face, I am strong in the Lord and in the power of His might. I know that I am an overcomer. I walk in confidence, courage, and peace, because my victory is not based on my strength but only on His power. I fight the good fight of faith through praise and worship because I have already won through Christ.

Prayer

Victorious God, thank You for always causing me to win and to triumph over the enemy. Because of the death and resurrection of Jesus Christ, I am free, redeemed, and empowered to overcome. Remind me daily that You are always there and that Your power is greater than any obstacle I face. Help me to walk in boldness, faith, and praise even in the midst of the battle, knowing that because of You, victory is already mine. Strengthen my heart, oh God, I fix my eyes on You, the One who never fails. In Jesus name, Amen.

Listen to this:
"Victory" by Yolanda Adams

"Pause and Ponder"

Declare your victory today and every day! It is not by your own might, or by your power, but by the power and promise of the Almighty One who has already won it all! Victory belongs to Jesus, and He gave it to you!

The key to victorious living isn't in your strength but in your submission to the Holy Spirit. Take today's scripture, "But thanks be to God! He causes us to triumph through Jesus Christ." (1 Corinthians 15:57). Declare your victory! Create your own melody, and sing the word of God!

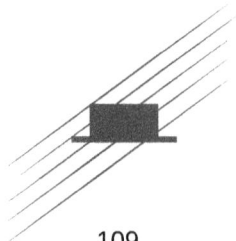

_____

_____

_____

_____

_____

_____

_____

_____

WORSHIP

W

"God is spirit, and those who worship Him must worship in spirit and truth."

John 4:24 NKJV

Understanding the Word

The word "worship" is profound, with a depth of meaning that has many layers, defying a single definition. It involves expressing deep respect, love and admiration, often demonstrated through a lifestyle of devotion.

It is expressed through adoration, obedience, reverence, and spiritual practices such as praying, singing, and acts of love and service. Ultimately, worship is a wholehearted response to the perceived worthiness of the object of our worship.

Selah Moment

We were created to worship God; our worship belongs to Him and Him alone. But to even begin to grasp what this means, it begins with giving our heart to Him and the journey of walking in the awareness of His presence, knowing His word and staying connected to Him. This relationship goes far beyond moments in a song, it is about living in a constant state of dependency on Him. It is a lifestyle that glorifies God through our thoughts, words, deeds, and attitudes. The enemy is after our worship. Just as he dared to tempt Jesus in the wilderness with power, fame, and earthly rewards in exchange for worship, he'll try the same with you. Stand firm! Fight back with the Word of God as Jesus did.

Declare with boldness: "My worship belongs to the Most High God and to Him alone." Obedience to God is our highest form of worship. Our obedience draws us closer to Him, restoring our souls, transforming us and filling us with His love, peace, and joy. It centers our lives on Him, reminding us that He is our Creator, Savior, and Sustainer, our Everything. As we worship, we grow in humility, letting go of self-centeredness and focusing on His glory and who He is.

God is looking for those who will worship Him in Spirit and in Truth. John 4:23 says, "But the time is coming, indeed it's here now, when true worshipers must worship the Father in spirit and in truth." Worship is knowing His truth; it involves studying and memorizing His word, so we do not fall into false worship. True worship is learned and practiced; it involves the whole person, spirit, soul, mind and body. It begins with the recognition of your total dependence on your Father God for your very existence.

Declaration

I choose to live a life of worship, being constantly aware of His presence, freely expressing my love, gratitude, and devotion to the Jehovah God, who is worthy of all honor, glory and praise. I am created to worship God in spirit and truth. My heart, mind, and soul are focused on honoring Him daily.

Prayer

Lord, I come before You with a heart of authentic worship. You are worthy of all my worship and adoration. Teach me to worship You with my whole being, not just in words but in the way I live each day. Help me to seek You sincerely, connecting with You in spirit and truth. Let my life be a reflection of Your love and glory, and may my worship draw me closer to You. I surrender all that I am to honor and glorify You. I worship ONLY You! In Jesus name, Amen.

Listen to this:
"Here I Am To Worship" by Maverick City Music
(feat. Ryan Ofei)

"Pause and Ponder"

We were created to worship the Lord. All throughout the day, meditate on the Lord and declare in your heart and mind, "I WORSHIP You and You alone." Actively listen to the Lord all day with every intention, thought, action, and Word, devoted to glorifying Him. Worship will lead us to a place of surrender, inviting God's presence and power into our daily lives.

EXCEEDINGLY

X

"Now to Him who is able to do exceedingly abundantly above all that we ask or think, according to the power that works in us..."

Ephesians 3:20 NKJV

Understanding the Word

E xceeding is a measure that is unlimited and divine. Exceedingly means to an extreme degree; far beyond what is usual or expected; to a very large degree. This word expresses something that goes beyond measure, overflowing, and surpassing. When used in Scripture, it often describes God's capacity to bless, provide, and move in supernatural ways.

Selah Moment

God is a generous God, the God of overflow, abundance and more than enough. His power is not confined by our limitations. When Paul uses the phrase "exceedingly, abundantly, above ALL..." He is saying that His goodness surpasses human logic. God is able to DO far beyond what our imagination can conceive. What an awesome God we serve! So, because God is exceedingly generous, shouldn't our worship reflect the same measure? Think of the woman with the alabaster box. She didn't just give Jesus a polite little offering; she gave her most valuable possession to Him, her absolute best, her everything. She gave her tears, her dignity and displayed an act of extreme love and honor for all to see. Some of the onlookers didn't understand that kind of worship, and they were offended, but Christ was moved by her sacrifice and love.

She gave us something that we must pay attention to and learn from. A powerful example of what extravagant love and devotion looks like. The kind of worship God deserves is: exceedingly, abundantly, above all...not half-hearted, not routine, not restrained, but extravagant, wholehearted worship, without limits. So don't hold back. Let your praise and worship overflow. Let it rise beyond the ordinary. Break your alabaster box today, give Him all you've got, pour out your most costly possession at His feet. He is worthy of your exceedingly abundant, above all, worship!

Declaration

God's power is working in me and through me. I believe He is able to do exceedingly, abundantly, above all I ask or imagine. I walk in expectation of His overflow and favor today. Because of this, I break the box of routine, and I pour out my heart in worship, freely and without reservation. Like the woman with the alabaster box, I give Him my best, I give Him my ALL.

Prayer

Today, Father, I bring You my best, a heart full of worship. You are my ONE desire, Lord. Thank You for being a generous God of more than enough. You said, "Ask and it shall be given. Seek and I will find." So I come to you in faith believing You for more. Your ways are higher, and Your power is limitless. I thank you for your goodness. You deserve more than a song. You deserve more than routine or what I have rehearsed. You deserve worship that is extravagant, passionate, and pure. May my life be an offering that reflects how great You truly are. In Jesus name, Amen.

Listen to this:
Exceedingly, Abundantly - Antonia Pecot / Suno

"Pause and Ponder"

Take time today to reflect on an area in your life where you have limited God. Ask Him to refresh your vision for your life and stretch your faith. Dream big! Write down the vision and make it plain and simple. Share it with someone today.

He doesn't just want to meet your needs, but He wants to exceed your desires and expectations, meet all of your needs, above and beyond what you could ask or think -- for His glory alone.

Acronym of True Worship

W - Willingness – Genesis 22:5

Willingness is saying "yes" to God and "no" to other desires.

O – Obedience –John 14:23

Obedience to God's word is the highest form of worship.

R – Reverence - Hebrews 12:28

Reverence is the fear of the Lord and the beginning of wisdom.

S – Servanthood – Psalms 100:2

A heart that worships God is a heart willing to serve others.

H – Humility – 1 Peter 5:6

Humility invites the presence of God because it creates a space where He alone is exalted.

I – Intelligence – Romans 12:2

Love the Lord with all our mind – Study, Meditate and memorize the word of God and BE TRANSFORMED .

P – Preparation – Proverbs 24:27

Preparation demonstrates our passion and commitment to obey the calling of God in our life.

W
O
R
S
H
I
P

YES

Y

"For all the promises of God in Him are Yes, and in Him Amen, to the glory of God through us."

2 Corinthians 1:20 NKJV

Understanding the Word

Yes is a word of agreement, surrender, and affirmation. In the life of a Believer, saying "yes" to God means yielding to His will, accepting His promises, and walking in obedience. The word "yes" activates God's purpose for our lives. It is a demonstration of faith that opens the door for God to move in and through us.

Selah Moment

Saying yes to God is an act of faith. It is a response to His love, His calling, and His purpose for our lives. Every time we say yes to the Lord, it is like flipping the switch; connecting to electricity! Just as a disconnected device cannot be powered, we are connected to God through faith and prayer to receive His divine power. This is when we step deeper into His way, His Spirit, and the life He has destined for us. God already said yes to us when He sent His Son, Jesus, to die on a cross for our sins. He said yes to our salvation, yes to grace, yes to love, and now He is inviting us to respond with our own yes.

This powerful *yes,* will require courage, sacrifice, and surrender, but will always leads to freedom, abundance and fruitfulness. It is not about perfection; it's about positioning and placing our heart and mind in a posture of availability.Saying yes to God daily invites His peace, provision, protection, power, His presence, and His promises into our lives.

Declaration

Today, I say yes to You, Lord. Yes to Your will. Yes to Your way. Yes to Your promises. I trust that Your plans for me are good, and I choose to follow You with a willing heart. My yes unlocks doors of faith, blessing, and purpose. I am available and ready to walk in all You have for me.

Prayer

Heavenly Father, thank You for saying yes to me through Your Son, Jesus. Thank You for Your promises that are always true. Today, I SAY a wholehearted YES to You, Lord! I say yes to Your will, yes to Your timing, and yes to Your leading. Even when I don't see the full picture, I trust You. Give me the strength and faith to keep saying yes, even when it is hard. Let my yes be yes, and let it be an act of worship and a declaration of my love for You. In Jesus name, Amen.

Listen to this:
"Trading My Sorrows" by Israel Houghton

"Pause and Ponder"

What is God asking you to say yes to today? Trust Him—it could be the beginning of something greater than you could ever imagine. Write it down...

ZEAL

Z

"Never be lacking in zeal, but keep your spiritual fervor, serving the Lord."

Romans 12:11 NIV

Understanding the Word

Zeal is divine energy that is passionate, devoted, enthusiastic, and fervent, especially in pursuing a cause or purpose. In the context of faith, being zealous means having a burning desire and enthusiasm to honor God that leads to action, and the power to serve Him with all our heart, soul, mind, and strength.

Selah Moment

"The zeal of God" refers to His passionate commitment to accomplish His purposes in the earth. It is a powerful force driven by the energy of His love and jealousy for us. God is a jealous God, and what He desires more than anything is exclusive worship from His people. God desires for His people to be hot or cold. Can you imagine craving a hot cup of coffee or tea, and when you put the cup to your mouth in anticipated pleasure, and it is lukewarm! How disappointing! Neither hot enough to satisfy nor cold enough to refresh — it's lifeless. In Revelation 3:16, Jesus speaks to the church, He said "Because you are lukewarm—neither hot nor cold—I am about to spit you out of My mouth." He isn't talking about temperature — He's talking about spiritual fervor. Lukewarm faith is faith that is indifferent or without committment; it is worship without wonder. It is when we sing songs but our hearts no longer burn with love for Him.

He wants us zealous and on fire for Him, for Him and Him alone.

This kind of zeal reflects a heart that is filled with gratitude, that has been touched deeply by the love of Christ. A heart that is engaging in the passionate pursuit of getting to know God and His word. It energizes our worship, fuels our prayers, and motivates us to serve Him and others with joy and purpose. As believers, we must be zealous in our faith, in service, and in our witness for Christ, even when facing opposition or hardship.

Zeal for God is not driven by emotion alone, but by truth and a sincere relationship with Him, loving Him with all our heart, soul, mind, and strength. It is a response to His goodness, mercy, and power in our lives. When we are zealous for the Lord, we reflect His heart and become a light in the world, inspiring others to pursue Him with the same passion.

God longs for hearts that are alive with passion, not indifferent, or just comfortable with routine. He desires worship that's hot — vibrant, wholehearted and intentional. When our love cools, our worship loses its fragrance. But when we stir the flame again, every act of praise becomes a fragrant offering that delights His heart.

Declaration

I am in a passionate pursuit of the Lord, to know and to love Him with my all. I will keep the consuming fire of zeal burning in my soul! An unwavering desire to see His will done in my life, to share His love and to see His name lifted high. I am full of passion and purpose in my worship and service to Him. My heart burns with love for God, and I pursue Him with all my strength. I will not grow weary in doing well, for His Spirit renews me daily. My life is a testimony of fervent devotion and joyful obedience.

Prayer

Lord Yeshua, ignite that holy fire within me. Fill me with zeal to serve You wholeheartedly, without hesitation or fear. Let my heart burn with a passion for Your Word, Your presence, and Your purpose. Remove any complacency or spiritual dullness and renew my spirit with joy and energy. Use my life to glorify You and help me to inspire others by the way I live, passionately expressing that zeal for Your kingdom. Let my worship burn hot with love, and my life overflow with gratitude and passion for You. In Jesus name, Amen.

Listen to this:
"Zeal" by The Belonging Co / All The Earth
(feat. Henry Seeley)

"Pause and Ponder"

Ask yourself this question "Has my worship grown routine or cold? This is the day to re-ignite your zeal and live boldly for His glory.

Write down the ways you can demonstrate your zeal for the Lord in your everyday life.

_____

_____

_____

_____

_____

_____

_____

_____

"WORSHIP IS THE SUBMISSION OF
ALL OF OUR NATURE TO GOD.

IT IS THE QUICKENING OF THE
CONSCIENCE BY HIS HOLINESS;
THE NOURISHMENT OF THE
MIND WITH HIS TRUTH;

THE PURIFYING OF IMAGINATION
BY HIS BEAUTY;
THE OPENING OF THE HEART
TO HIS LOVE;

THE SURRENDER OF WILL
TO HIS PURPOSE--
ALL THIS GATHERED UP
IN ADORATION,
THE MOST SELFLESS EMOTION OF
WHICH OUR NATURE IS CAPABLE."

— WILLIAM TEMPLE

CONCLUSION

Worship doesn't end when the music fades or the final page is turned. It lives and breathes in your daily surrender, your quiet moments with God, and the words you choose to speak, sing, and believe.

This devotional may have walked you from "Abide" to "Zeal," but your journey through the language of worship has only just begun. The words explored here are not an end—they are an invitation. An invitation to continue cultivating a heart that speaks the language of heaven. To search the Scriptures with fresh eyes. To ask the Holy Spirit to illuminate new truths. To sing with greater understanding. To pray with deeper clarity.
To live from a place of abiding wonder.

Let your life be a living "Worship Word." You are an expression of His glory on the earth. Whenever the noise of life tries to drown out your devotion, remember this rhythm:

Pause. Reflect. Selah. Worship and repeat...

When worship is grounded in the study of His Word and flows from a deep understanding, it doesn't just stay on the surface, it flows into every part of who you are, it becomes more than expression, it becomes transformation. Keep learning the words that matter to God. Keep practicing His presence through praise. Keep letting your worship flow from meditation and revelation.

Never lose the wonder of His presence.

ABOUT THE AUTHOR

Antonia Pecot is a worship leader, coach, singer, songwriter, and recording artist with over 25 years of experience equipping the local church. Guided by Proverbs 11:25—"Those who refresh others will themselves be refreshed"—she lives to pour into others, and her mission is clear: to cultivate the heart of true worship in every believer.

As the founder of **Fresh Rain Music**, Antonia provides practical and spiritual development for worship teams through leadership coaching, workshops, consulting, and customized training resources. Her mission is to help churches strengthen and unify their worship ministries by teaching principles of servant leadership, vocal confidence, stage presence, spiritual maturity, and creative excellence.

Antonia's journey has taken her from intimate church gatherings to large-scale ministry platforms across the United States and abroad. She has faithfully served in diverse settings—church plants, multicultural ministries, and established congregations—where she continues to equip leaders to embrace worship as both art and assignment.

Her rich history of collaboration includes partnerships with respected ministries such as Victory World Church, City Church, Fellowship Bible Church, and Eagles Nest Church, as well as renowned worship artists like Israel Houghton, Martha Munizzi, Babbie Mason, and Darlene Zschech. She has also recorded six original worship projects, each reflecting her deep passion for authentic, Spirit-led worship.

Born in England, raised in Canada, and rooted in her Jamaican heritage, Antonia brings a global voice and perspective to worship that transcends culture, denomination, and tradition. She now resides in Atlanta, Georgia, where she continues to write, mentor, and lead worship while developing new initiatives under the Fresh Rain brand—including her devotional series, "Worship Word of the Day."

Above all, Antonia's greatest joy is seeing lives transformed through worship and purpose awakened through the presence of God. She is also a proud mother of six amazing adult children and grandchildren who continue to inspire her faith and legacy.

To contact Antonia--
Fresh Rain Music LLC
Website: freshrainworship.com
Email : info@freshrainworship.com
Phone # 770-322-4415

"I've had the privilege of knowing Antonia Pecot for over 30 years, and I can say without hesitation that she is one of the most gifted and anointed worship leaders I've ever met. Antonia played a foundational role in the early years of Eagles Nest Church, leading our Worship and Arts Department with excellence, passion, and a deep love for God. In Worship Word of the Day, she pours out decades of wisdom, revelation, and experience into a devotional journey that will inspire worshippers, equip leaders, and draw hearts closer to God. This book is more than a resource — it's a refreshing well for every believer who desires to worship God in spirit and in truth."

Pastor Lee Allen Jenkins, Founder & Senior Pastor
Eagles Nest Church, Roswell, GA

Antonia Pecot is a true vessel of worship—an anointed leader, teacher, and mentor whose life reflects a deep devotion to God and a passion for excellence in ministry. Through her years of service, she has inspired countless worshipers, musicians, and leaders to pursue both skill and surrender in their callings. Her ministry extends far beyond the platform; whether guiding a worship team, training volunteers, or conducting powerful seminars, Antonia brings a rare blend of musical mastery and spiritual sensitivity, carrying an understanding of worship that transcends performance and ushers others into the presence of God.

Bishop Tony Evans, Pastor
Connection Point Church, Austell, GA

www.ingramcontent.com/pod-product-compliance
Lightning Source LLC
Chambersburg PA
CBHW070457090426
42735CB00012B/2589